VOICES & VENUES
In VERSE!

XIV

By -
Kenneth J. Hesterberg

ISBN 978-1-62806-305-9

Library of Congress Control Number 2020923150

Published by Salt Water Media
29 Broad Street, Suite 104
Berlin, MD 21811
www.saltwatermedia.com

Cover photo, courtesy of:
P/Lt/C Niles J. Simpson III, Cambridge Sail and Power Squadron

Primary Editor: Janet Jones

When letters were Numbers!!

In those days,
When speaking Latin, Roman Legions,
Ruled, most of the then, known world!
When much of thought & writing,
Followed what those in Greece,
Had set into motion!

Before, Arabic Numbers were in vogue!
Romans, used upper case letters,
To establish a counting system!
With no "Zeros" to be seen!
When if "I," was before a letter__
Meant less, or if after was more!

When a "V", meant 5 and "X" meant 10, and "L" was 50,
And "C" 100, and "D" 500, and "M" a 1,000__
And then "C" did the same as "I" with "D" or "M!"
And, the known world, with letters did count!

"XIV"

Is the fourteenth Book, in the:
VOICES & VENUES IN VERSE series,
Of Short Stories in Verse__
To temp intellect, and memory,
And perhaps, set your thinking into motion!

Fourteen__ a Fortnight,
Fourteen, in days, 1/26 of a year!
XIV, time to find thoughts, to you that appear!

Ψ

Dedication

If we be honest, and thinking put to task,
There would be factually thousands,
Who in one-way or another,
Have touched upon our lives__
For good or bad, an imprint made!
In reality to name one or some,
Is a disservice to the many!
So in humble gratitude,
I say, Thank You!
One and All!
For time,
Known
Or not,
A gift,
Shared,
That most likely passed on,
To the many whom I have touched,
A toast to each and everyone!

Ψ

"XIV"

Still in vogue,
After 2,000 years,
Not daily used, but for specialties chosen!

To and for me,
This Book the fourteenth is special!
It is well beyond,
The number of books,
I first thought to write!
Note, it is not a novel,
To read and then shelve,
But a small tome, a good book,
To read or reread, during your life!

Table of Contents

Books by KJH in the series: VOICES & VENUES IN VERSE!

The World of Water
Fair winds and foul, beacons, lighthouses, on ocean, rivers & bays, or in the deep!
Yesterdays, Other Days and Holidays
Holidays of humankind, Tributes, Recognitions & Remembrances!
Inspiration
Thoughts the additive, for the engine of humankind!
Inspiration Two & too!
Self-motivation through life!
Moments in Time and Scope!
Memories, ideas, capacity for achievement, vastness for self!
Of People and Spaces!
Space like most things in life, only a restriction of the human self!
Choices, Chances & Life!
Choices- to make! Chances__ one takes! Life__ a gift of worth!
VISTAS!
Visions of the beholder, seen, felt & sensed, memory markers!
"Tapestry" of Life Spun!
Woven through ones life, how good when done, depends on the path chosen!
"Earth Tones!"
Majestic in color & sound, there, where ere you go__ your gift!
"Earth Rhythms!"
Earth's rhythms playing on this planet's scene, there to grab and hold!
"Rebound"
A skill to perfect, to better your life!
"Baker's Dozen!"
When a dozen becomes 13, short stories in Verse, touching heart, soul and mind!
"XIV"
A tribute to days when numbers, were letters, and no zeros could be found!

Written and awaiting publication!
"Intuition!"
Perhaps a touch of magic, or ESP, or remnants found in one's DNA!
"Turns"
Actions that influence the direction of life!
"Mélange"
"This, that and the other", to capture your invested moments!
"Diversity"
Life's colors, sounds, feelings and times!
"The Gathering:"
Of, a like group, human and none human, together find a kindred ship!

All cover photos are waters near the Chesapeake Bay__
my muse since childhood.

The verses "Short Stories" meant to be read, throughout life!

Prologue

What to include in this book?
Lots of potential material, now ready!
So much still coming from the past,
And, so much, happening in "Today's World!"

The right selection of content__
Of Verse is always a conundrum!
For unlike a periodical, or a newscast,
A book takes time,
And much of the copy is dated__
And somewhat historical,
By the time it is read!

Even if, a retrospective, a collection of new facts,
Fresh approaches to a situation old__
The challenge is, always, to get the reader to read!

My books, are short or longer stories in Verse__
To be read and reread through out one's life!
Hopefully help the reader__
To recapture old memories,
And, stir new ideas__ things to try!

It is my hope that I have accomplished,
What I have set out to do!
And, all meets the readers' needs and expectations!
My very best, I wish to readers one and all!

Ψ

On Loan!

There is a wise old adage:
"Waste not, Want Not!"
Truly relevant, when referring__
To the "Birth Gift of TIME!"

Granted with an unknown__
Expiration date!
Time, that you get__
Is what you got!
You can't: buy, steal or beg more!
You can massage it!
You can make good use of it!
Or lose it, through stupidity for sure!

But, when it's up__ you are down!
Just a mound on the ground!
So panic not, for you be judged__
On how, you made, every second of it count!

Time__ is worth more than diamonds or gold!
Doesn't mean, being busy every minute__
But the wise among us,
Never, ever, willingly__ fritter it away!
Yes, time and the twins__
Of breath and health, are the greatest of gifts!
Without them, you cannot last__
Even seconds of a day!

Be wise; utilize every morsel gifted to you!
The worse thing one can say is:
I wish I had___!

Ψ

The World of Now!

Each new generation,
Opens up, its new world!
Sure, past generations, have laid__
Stepping stones, based on their knowledge__
Of the past,
And what they had learned!
But the young have a vision of the future__
That many times,
The past, could never glean!

But what I have learned,
As the years, have ganged up on me__
Was I should have asked,
More questions,
And even more-so, listened, to the elders,
That had surrounded me!
For there was, wisdom to capture__
After separating the wheat from the chaff!
But so little written__ lost now, to posterity!

Funny, how we get smarter,
When so much time, was wasted; lost,
And life now, has slowed us down__
In too many ways to count!
But now there are *computers*,
Packed with, and being inundated__
With facts to find!
Question: are we out-smarting humankind?
Will, this be_ ours to see_ mankind's fatal crime!

Ψ

Spring into Life!

There was a "spring'
By the road side,
Running from a two inch pipe,
For, how long, few cared to guess!

The water cold and sparkling clear,
And, people stopped by,
In day and night,

To grab a cup full,
Or to fill a jug or thrice!

How many years,
No one could find a clue!
Who truly knew?

But rumor had it,
Buckskin men and Native Americans,
Stopped on their travels too!

The pipe some said,
That the CCC set it, in 1934?
And, many Boy Scouts, now old men,
Remembered the spring,
Back when "campaign hats" they wore!

And, of course one day,
A government Bureaucrat,
Thought it a traffic hazard!

And, said that would never do,
And, had the pipe removed!

Well, that, so-in-so, had no idea,
What a hornet's nest,
He had begun to brew!

And in the next election,
His boss was dumped,
And, the new guy, who used the spring,
Showed that feller to the door!

So now the "spring" is running again,
And there is a road off the main,
And a nice parking spot,

With tables and benches,
And, there is a group__ who makes sure,
Everything stays "ship shape" there!

It doesn't pay __to get the locals__
Too riled up__ you hear?
For who knows, who knows__

The right people,
Who can get things done!
And, get "problems" shown to the door!

To bad, too many other things,
Just like the spring,
Have been tossed, by those__
Who could not see beyond their nose!

And, me I'll not tell where,
That spring be there__
Cause, you could be one of those!

Ψ

Day of Reckoning!

Waiting, we cannot afford to do!
But many will__
Claiming political correctness!
Or, racial discrimination!
Then, waiting too long, and lose__
Much, in the way, better too choose!

Will we, but continue to sit back,
And, just watch__
This country, this "Republic" of ours,
The best in the world___
Go down the tubes!
Because, action we didn't take?

Buried in plastic trash!
Drinking polluted water!
Tasting lead, from pipes, eaten away!
Breathing smog filled air__
Because the EPA functions not!
Is this to be, what tomorrow will stay?

We put up with sociopaths__
Who find ways, to use the airwaves!
Petrochemicals in the land, air and sea!
Drug companies foisting harmful pills__
On the elderly and the addicts__
For outrageous dollars they see!

Illegals eating at our economy!
The 1%__ stealing money.
Using, tax codes, there, like devised!
Money that should be supporting the USA!

Gangs, getting away,
With, murder, robbery, rape & more!

Some politicians,
Bending the Constitution to their whims!
How much time do we have?
This list is endless! Is it any wonder__?
A revolution is fermenting!
Let's not be too late, changes to impose!

Alternatives, our conscience already knows!
These lines touch on a few challenges,
Just a few of our woes!

This was one nation, one language,
One code__ the Constitution!
That our ancestor's, facing death, did propose!

Yes, we treated the Red Man wrong,
And we had slavery__ despicable!
But that came from history, millenniums ago__
From other countries our ancestors did know!
Pure stupidity__ we 200 years ago, let grow!
And things, so opposite the "Golden Rule!"

People__ Stop Vacillating!
How soon "rogue nations"
Will be breaking down our doors?

If we do not, fix the wrongs,
We for centuries have ignored__
Once a great nation__ will be no more!

Is this the legacy you will leave__
For generations not yet born?

Ψ

That Organization!

Every Organization is like a chain__
Only as strong, as its weakest link! Link__ the alias for Member!
There are three types of members:

Do Nothings: Too busy, too old, too young,
Too tired, or don't give a damn!
Do Something: Leery of responsibility
Little time but give it a shot,
Tell me (show me) How and what to do!
The Do Everything: needs to be involved,
Makes the time necessary, politically motivated,
Ego_ nobody else will do it, Lets get it done!

There are three types of Associations:
Weak, dying or dead;
Is where, the "Do Nothings" out-number the other Do's!

Holding or crawling:
Is, where the "Do Something's" out-number the other two, Do's!

Growing & Super:
Is where the "**Do Everything's**"
Understand the other two Dos, and involves them!
Does empathize and recognize them!
And moves the other two Do's__ to do!

Think this not true?
Then honestly analyze your organization__
And, then take the appropriate action!
Longevity requires all to do! Remember, baby sitters get paid!
These words are more truth than fiction!

Ψ

Common Sense Required!

As I sat looking out of windows clear__
Counting__ seventeen days,
As the Equinox, draws near!
Crazy weather have seen,
For the last year or more!
Here and everywhere!

Yes, but will say__ we here on Delmarva,
Have fared better, than so many others!
Except for rain, the farmer's bane!

So no moans with you will I share!
But prayers, for God's
Help, for others__ everywhere!

But for what has happened,
And what is forecast, to come,
Can only say__ only fools today__
Would say, there is,
"No Global Warming," at play!
But, hopefully there is time, to overcome!

If all peoples of the world,
Soon__ do not stand together__
As caretakers of the Earth,
And, put personal grievances__ aside

Chances are__ humankind;
A new place__ must find to reside!

Or wonder__, who will be the last,
Into oblivion__ to slide!

Ψ

Saturday Morning!

A busy Saturday @ PK's Restaurant!
The Garden Room near full.

With, lots of conversation__
And me getting ideas,
For words in verse to jot down!

Always ideas found, just listening around!

To my left a family of four,
Their youngest boy, about 6 and a half,
The older, no age claimed,
But two or three years more!

And as usual fun to watch,
As mom and I winked,
A time or more__
At the conversation of the boys!

To my right was a couple,
And, we shared a laugh,
They too, were watching also,
The antics of the boys!

Diagonally__ six were sitting at a table,
One, twenty something a male,
And, five women, three generations!
No pause in the chatter!

The "guy" just shoveled his food down!
Moral—Eat alone!
Or have more males in the crowd!

But, parts of conversation, my ear did find!

I chatted with one of the waitresses,
To see if she had started,
One of my books, I had gifted to her,
Her reply was such:

"I will, I want to, said she,
But, first I've got to get,
My Christmas down!"
It was the last week__ in January?

I kept tuned in on the conversations around!
As my breakfast, disappeared!
Yes, a great spot on a Saturday morning__
Who knows, what you will see or hear!

And, most times__
Great ideas for a new verse I find!
Ideas others shared, without being aware,
All for under 10-bucks including tip!

Yes, I love eating in the Garden Room,
With a good view of the retaining pond,
And all of nature's action there around,
The birds & cold out, and the people inside!

Ψ

Truth Behold!

It is amazing, how much the brain, can hold__
It is sort of like the "computer cloud."
So the more you learn and store away,
The more space__ is always found!

Ψ

A Time Remembered!

I remember many days,
When out, our kitchen window gazed__
And, could see deer__
Munching apples under that, tree!

They, were always welcome guests,
As long as they left, my pear tree alone!
And, this day even more so,
Because, they had two fawns in tow!

Ruth and I moved quietly,
To the screened-in porch,
To better watch these tiny things,
And, finally, moved outside!

We, sat upon a bench,
As we had done many times before!
The deer we think knew us well,
For one was on the ground, just watching!

Soon, the fawns, moved, our way!
The doe got up and watched,
And, my bride, knelt down,
And, quietly waited!

And, closer came the trio now,
My bride, slowing stretched our her hand,
I, a move did not take,
As those, little ones, a friend did make!

After a bit, they quietly moved away!
It always amazed me,
The "touch" my lady had!
We knew our guest, again would return!

Too bad, the apples,
For only a few weeks stayed!
Twas an experience we missed,
When we moved, those 100s of miles away!

Ψ

Maybe!

It doesn't take long, for one too learn,
Life and living is full of twists and turns!

Some take one, into darkness,
But more "thank heaven," into sunlight!
Many times, that choice is yours to make.

But, there are times,
When no other course is yours, to do__
Then, tis character__ that comes through!

Life, and living, gets one to realize__
Learning and getting knowledge and experience,
Is, essential; and a never ending challenge__
If, you wish to do__ all you dream to do!

Stating, a bit of common sense:
Prior, planning, prevents,
Punk, poor performance!
Perhaps new or you knew before?
But, hopefully now a part of your DNA!

Just thoughts to help you along life's way!

Ψ

Come a Weekend!

There is a place I like too go,
This place a particular, food purveyor,
Full of life, and conversation to know!
And me, a chance to hear, write and grow!

Here within, is good food, and much banter,
And, if one listens many good stories,
One can take in!
And I get many ideas, for Verse I can begin!

But, if the noise gets too great,
Or, the conversation to boisterously loud,
I can walk out with a smile,
Or if irritated__ tell someone to lower it!

Being an old curmudgeon,
Only get dirty looks, and no fisticuffs__
With which, do not have to contend,
And, at times, have gotten, applause!

Now, I eat here quite often,
Somewhat a regular I am!
The waitresses know me as a tipper,
And, off times loan me a pen!

For if things are going well,
I turn the place mat over,
And with their pen (mine forgotten),
Stories in Verse do draft!

On this one day, I'm remembering,
Two elders (still working),
But retirement, not far away,
Both eating and talking, had a lot to say!

Both in flannel and ball caps,
And both, by twang, Eastern Shore men!
Were talking of driving__
Trucks hauling chickens each day!

And the wear and tare,
On trucks and their bodies,
No longer young, a game to play__
But, neither ready, to call it a day!

And, at another, close by table,
A foursome, two, much older__
And the other two,
So much less, in years that day!

The younger talking of Aruba,
The elders, smiling, at each other,
And me think, the elders__
Just happy, to share time, this way!

Sometimes I hear stories of valor,
Sometimes about kids moved away,
Sometimes, it's history never written,
All the time, verse I want to put into play!

To God, I send my gratitude,
For an ear, to listen intently,
And, for verse to ink__
Into books to write, and each day to see!

Not a bad life__
For a guy, now alone,
With much gray that is shown!
But still breath__ that comes my way!

And, finding a little talent, on life's way!
And, a chance to help__ some not-for-profits,
With the profits, I get__
From book signing, and sales!

Take a moment and think about you!
When you wake each morning,
And, life isn't yet through__
Find something good, to help others,
Which will make you__ feel good too!

Ψ

Honest Appraisal!

I have great memories,
Rooted in all four seasons,
That I have been, blessed to see!

And, oh so pleased, with the details__
As my memories return to me!
And, must also say,
I love each moment, of those yesterdays!

And, do hope and pray,
There are many more times awaiting__
For an even and older me!

But in honesty, must state truly__
Fall, autumn__ is my, and ever will be,
Favorite, of times and life to see!

Ψ

A Guest, Not Wanted!

Too many gifts, from Mr. Arthur Ritis,
And, when he arrives,
It's, like the coming, of unwanted guest__
And, leaving__ is a time he won't discuss!

He is a rotten guy to know,
Always hanging about,
A true pain where ever,
And he ruins__
Much of one's life__ forever!

I pray Mr. Arthur__
Has, better things to do,
Than to spend his time chasing you!
For he is a real "bastard" and SOB __
And, I am here to suggest, evade him__
For truly, he, you don't want to see!

And, if you don't believe me,
And let him come to call,
Don't knock on my door,
Just keep crying,
And walking, down the hall!

Advice given!
Take you not__
And pay the price,
For "stupid" you then, have got!
This prayer, I send to many_
Too bad, they listen not!
Will you__ I pray?
AMEN!

Ψ

Between the Eves!

Sitting, I was, tea mug, now half empty__
Thinking of my family, homeward bound!
Christmas behind,
And New Years Eve, 3 days away!

Son Paul, his 52nd birthday,
On the 29th as they get home!
The girls, just days away,
From their birthdays,
But daughter-in-law Dee and I,
Are September celebrants!

Come the first of 2018,
The youngest granddaughter's 11th Birthday!
Wasn't it, just yesterday__?
Her first, steps taken, at her first Christmas?
I like to think, it was a gift__
For, her great-grandmother__
Who we lost, just days before her 1st!

On the 9th, the eldest will be 19,
Almost__ as tall, as I am,
High School near done,
College entrance, already won!
How my now gone bride, would have smiled,
At this young woman, blossomed out!

I know, it has been said times before__
"Where did the time go?"
But, here at Mimi's house,
Just a day ago, that Red head,
In the evening, on the phone with her beau!
The days of dolls and such,
Never again to know!
Can' t help thinking,

This, was my wife's, favorite holiday!
How, she loved to be with our family!
Hey, this isn't a downer__
It's, just capturing some moments,
Now gone, and new ones coming!

You know, life is ever changing!
And mine not yet done,
With much left, I want to do!
I keep plugging on a legacy__
I think, everyone, should leave a legacy__
For those left behind—don't you?

And, this is life, I contend__
No next day is guaranteed,
Just proves__ time is a gift!
To be used to its fullest__
Waste a moment, and lose a memory!

Don't lose an opportunity,
Chances are, most never to be seen again!
And, as bad, as sometimes__ seems to be:
Live and reach out, for tomorrow__
It is then, more life__ yours to see!
For as long, as life, is granted to thee!
Grab hold, and go for the ride!

Ψ

To answer: is indeed, perhaps a need?
To inflate, an ego flagging!
Is this different, from trying to hold up__
A, big belly; which is sagging?

Ψ

All Hollows Year!

Midnight: the witching hour__
So, we are told!
Why this moment and not another--
Are ghost and goblins that particular?
Or is it__ just Satan, causing trouble!

Or when you were young__
To put a bit of fear into you!
Or, because the hands of a clock,
Are straight up, and not down?
Or is it just stories,
Like those now in the Bible,
That generations told, before written down?

The witching hour,
Chiming in a new day to be found!
Come daylight, when goblins and ghost,
And even witches and warlocks__
Never want to be found!

Do you believe__
Things you cannot see__
Are, watching you __
From the sky and ground?
And the "dead," will come back,
To take their pound of flesh,
For, bad things, you've hidden around?

Ah, the Witching Hour__
Just a Roman XII or not!
Or a time, <u>*YOU*</u> should fear a lot?
Perhaps, its time___
To, check your conscience out!
Or, take the Devil's hand, as time runs out?

Midnight comes on every night,
Not just Halloween!
Start, counting, the ghosts you have, seen!
Who come around to haunt your dreams!
But, are they dreams?

Maybe it's not too late__ too be good,
But know, Hades__ " ain't" that far below!
And, at some stroke of midnight,
Even, "goodie-two-shoes,"
Are called up__ or go down below!

"Ain't" the macabre, a kick to know?
Tell me now, you don't, believe it so!

Ψ

Let's Consider!

Dollars to donuts,
A saying old, that does, make sense!
Its derivation__ I can't say!

But, I am willing to bet___
Without dollars, no fatter do you get!
No really__ me thinks__

It tells you, that donuts can't match,
What dollars portend!

So, eat less__ donuts,
And, fewer dollars you spend!

Ψ

Another Day!

(A Day in the Life of a Verse-ist
Never the same, but hopefully still in the game)

Busy morning, creative editing of Book 11__
"Rhythms," publishing date__ unknown)
Drafted a letter to a friend,
On the death of her husband!
Knocked out the normal housework,
All mine__ since my bride passed on!

Up and down and moving around,
What these days__ I call exercise!

Rained heavy, all night,
And, was raw and cold,
Who, would believe,
Spring, was just weeks away!
As, I started to my Saturday,
Breakfast Place__
Another weekend__ had truly begun!

Before backing out of the drive,
I looked around!

The yard, looked like, pure wetlands,
Leaves, matted grass down, bare spots__
Where the squirrels had dug around!
I wonder if spring will ever come?

Got settled in PK's Garden room,
My favorite spot, to eat and look out!
The retention pond across the street,
The Cat "O" Nine Tail's, are old and brown!
Sad thing to see at near winter's end!
Can't wait till the new season begins!

Chatted with the girls,
And put my order in!
The pot of tea and glass of water,
Were already in place,
If I, ever changed, I'd throw_
The whole process out of pace!

As usual, I turned the placemat over,
Folded it into quarters, and began to write!
There was always within the crowd,
Who on weekends, breakfast ate_
Good material for verse to write!

Yes, this was my place,
Homey, busy, good folks,
Working the different jobs here!
And, an Oasis for ideas in books to fill!
Here friends to see_ and for a time_
Any sadness does flee!

And, I even dine on Creamed Chip Beef,
That was my wife's favorite!
But, in days, gone bye, never mine!
Funny, how taste buds change, or mature?
You'll excuse me now,
There is a verse to write_ my delight!

Just a bit of life,
For, an older guy without a wife,
Who is truly enjoying what he is doing,
And working to bring a little joy to others!
Try one of my books_
That will, guarantee, to bring me joy!

Ψ

Words, About Words!

Now hear what I say__
For what I say may help you__

Or not!

For I have determined,
That: "**then** and **than**," and "**to** and **too**",
Are, the most ego deflating pairs__
Of words, most humans can review!

When I use "then," you can bet__
It should have been "than!"
And, when I use "too,"
"To," should have been used!

Yes, these four words,
Abuse, miss use, and confound,
The likes of me__
In daytime, and nighttime,
And, most likely will, throughout eternity!

So, when, I become King,
(If that, be, my fate)
I will use whichever one,
I damn well want to/too!
So put that in your pipe and smoke it!

Of course, either one you may then/than also choose!
For I have pity on everyone,
Who using English grammar,
Has "to/too" over these words__ do stammer!

Ψ

Ponder!

I killed a fly the other day!
It wasn't that I didn't want to share____
My soup, with him or her!

It was just that the fly__
Was like too many in the world today,
Trying to steal, part of my life away.

It was, Just another, useless piece of stuff,
Doing little good__
And thought, I would look the other way!

Turn the other cheek, the bible says!
I surely will and would,
For those__ willing, to work each day!

The Bible says:
The meek will inherit the Earth,
Must be talking about "after death."

For look around the world,
The meek__
Are disappearing with each breath!

I find that fly,
Like, too damn many people today__
Annoying you, with nothing to say!

Too bad we can't swat__
Those two-legged flies,
I sure would, if the lawyers stayed away!

Ψ

Thoughts of Affection!

Now there are only two kinds of love,
And don't you ever forget it.

The first is governed,
By chemistry and emotion__
And, can last for days or even generations!

For some, perhaps, even of the same gender,
And, many think of love__
When hoping for, cohabitation!
Or, love of family__ without predetermination!

Now the second type of love,
Can actually be, a partner, of the first__
But need not be__ but be, truly a separate entity!

And, this one is founded__
On common sense and deep admiration!
Of one or some, form of recognition,
That there is bond created,
Nothing to do with sexual orientation!
Or the need for that type of gratification!
But, **of mutual, acceptance and understanding!**

That there is an affinity, which when fostered,
Will only with few exceptions,
Cause, a separation of mutual concurrence__

Whether they are near, or far__
That over and over again,
Be regenerated, and rekindled,
When a thought, or a call be unrehearsed

These are Loves, of two distinct amalgamations!
Either separated or compounded,
Seen, in the human, and animal kingdoms__
Many times a lifetime founded!
That carries through death or conflagration!

Now here perhaps an explanation,
Of what some frivolously call love!
Note the small letter "l."
And, is truly a "Horn Dog" reaction,
To a purely, sexual attraction__
For sexual satisfaction!

Found in both genders __
Of the human population!
Enough said, till "one" is dead__
Then, the other tries another direction!

See how simple, the explanation, can become__
Of what was a complicated function!

Maybe, even a truthful application,
Of the two types of love__
Can and do, serve both situations!
Ah Love; a most complicated emotion!

Ψ

A Thought to Subscribe!

"Keep the Faith! Is, more than just words__
It is a "State of Mind!"
Brought forth (me thinks) by those,
With the tenacity, to survive!

Ψ

Honest Judgments!

By watching and listening__
I have noted__ if one lives long enough,
There are times,
When insight, is most persistent!

Acceptance of what is presented,
Is a gift in its way!
Good, bad, or, of consequence__
But requires, a full examination__
To be truly consistent!

Details reviewed and cogitated,
But, if not all is comprehended__
One has no right to express,
Any biases__ intended!

Can one, put aside, a personal bias
And, make an unprejudiced judgment?
Or, is that beyond, most ability of humankind?
The answer to this__ is truly, a conundrum!

And, the willingness of one__
To truly face an enigma,
That baffles long held premise,
Perhaps, are thoughts, never to be fully extended!

What a world__ this could be,
If all exercised a process,
Of fair Judgment;
In all things faced in daily contention!

QED!

Ψ

Nature's Music!

The music of nature,
Takes many forms,
Sounds, tones, beats, rhythms,
And voices there, to project!

If one sits away in solitude,
And, cancels out, the cacophony of life,
An enters into a world, of ambient silence__
What heard; can be a symphony of delight!

From whence does this music come?
Why, from everything, and everywhere!
The song of birds, the roar of lions,
Prairie grass in the wind!

The crash of waves, thunder, lightening,
The movement of paws, hooves,
And the buzz of bees,
Waterfalls, volcanoes, and plate movement!

Everything is an item of sound,
Even in its' silence! The cooing of doves,
And, the chatter__ of a newborn!

Even the deaf, hear the music of their mind!

Grow in wisdom, tune in and on,
And to the music about you!
Take the time,
To, hear, Nature, singing to you!

A better person, you will become!

Ψ

Morbid, No, Just Life!

Should tomorrow, never come__
Then pain, sorrow and death__ are done!

And, so is your__
Life, family, fun and love!

All, you now can do, is hope,
The best in all things, you did.

Were, the very best you could do__
Throughout the life, you lived!

For, this, is part of the legacy
You, leave behind!

Memories good__ for those, who grieve!
And, ideas for all to share!

The more you do,
To prepare for that last day—

The better the remembrance,
Those, that are left, will praise!

So leave no debts, unpaid,
Clean your attic of junk arrayed!

Tell all, how much you did care,
Leave not, any uncertainty in the air!

Think of a keepsake, to leave for all,
And, a note to say, how much they ment to you__
For the friendship, in time, they gave!

These are just some thoughts,
For you to peruse!

But remember, wait not for the last__ to do,
Then fewer chores, on others will you impose!

If most is done, when you go,
And, what is left; requires, little yet to do,

That makes you,
Quite special; that's who!

Perhaps, to think, maybe, death is life's next step__
Would that not be nice to know?

Perhaps you will be the one__ to let the living know!

Ψ

A Thought to Keep!

Life (good or bad), happens__
And remains until the last breath ceases!

But, bones, not destroyed, by fire,
Age on and on, unless ground to dust!

Once in a while, a body in tact__
Is found, many 1000 or more years old!

This is a gift, from and unknown donor,
For us, to learn more, about days of those!

Ψ

A Kite in the Wind!

In time,
There is no more time,
For time is a borrowed thing,
Received at the time of birth,
And loaned till the time is denied.
With and expiration date unknown!
But comes with a test, to see__
How well, you use that gift!
And whether, should__
Have gotten any at all!
What test grade__
Will you get?
Maybe
Failing,
A bad,
Thing!
And in,
Satan's
Keep,
A next
Trip,
Will
See
?
Worth the time now,
To, explore your past?
And, make changes, as a timely thing__
Like a kite, on a string,
It takes work, to fly,
As does, everything!

Ψ

Parameters of Aging!

Aging is a path well made,
It happens to all things,
Before their final day!

Why it was deemed to be this way__
Perhaps happenstance,
But with much thought,
When life's plan was laid!

No lives, animate or inanimate,
Are exactly the same!

While the same species,
Maybe an average__ time to see!

Or longer or shorter, can be!
But each as a species__
A somewhat extent of time,
But not guaranteed!
For Nature__ at times, is a referee!

Inborn it seems,
Some things, demise__ will fight!

For most become enamored with life!
And innately understand,
One life__ is all you get!

And that, is not enough__
To see the wrong and right!
So take the opportunity__
To live__ every minute of life!

Ψ

Believing or Belief!

I don't know, if there is a God,
But I believe,
There is something out there!

It could be an alien form,
Who visited, even a million years ago__
Who appointed, Mother Nature__
To make the Earth_ just so!
I don't know!

I don't know if Jesus,
Is, the son, of God!
But I believe,
Someone special did trod,
The hills and valleys,
2,000 years ago!

After men had scribed
The Old Testament,
On parchment, to make it so!
But, I don't truly know!

Now, I've been to Church,
And, to Sunday school,
And put my finger prints on the Bible,
But only a few of its verses know!

And do I believe it all__
My answer would have to be no!
For too many humans,
Wrote passages, of what they thought,
Of those oral storytellers,
Who passed lore on down,
And had added things, never,
Known or found!

And there were the politicians, & others,
Who put there: "two cents worth" in__
For they, had another "cat to skin!"
And, others who,
Pitted one religion against another,
For a War to win!

But I, sort of keep the faith,
By accepting a passage,
That makes sense to me!
Many call it the Golden Rule__
Tis__ **"Do unto others,**
As you would have them,
Do unto you!"
If all people, would do that__
Me thinks__
The best of worlds, we could see!

Now, I am not saying,
I always walk a straight line!
But I sure try__ to do,
Much of my earthly time!
And it bothers me,
When, I don't__ and inside I cry!

We wouldn't need laws,
Or prisons, or have war,
And so much more,
If all did truly try,
To live, that Golden Rule!

Unfortunately, most Humankind,
Won't give it a try!
Must stop now, for the tears are in my eyes!

Ψ

More at PKs!

It was, still in time for Breakfast!
The place gearing up for__
The after church crowd,
But Breakfast there__ is my thing!
Which should carry me to dinnertime!

Lots of seating, in the Garden Room,
On this winter Sunday morn!
Between the meal times,
So, not as much conversation,
So less "fodder" for verse to write!

There was a foursome,
Sitting behind me,
With a child of three or four__
With eyes so blue,
That would put the sky to shame!

A true live wire, was she__
With, a smile,
That would melt an ice cycle!

It's always fun,
Eating in the Garden Room,
With a view of the pond, across the street!
And kiddos here, I love to watch,
How they reacted when eating out!

Much you can tell about parents,
If you watch the children,
And listen closely what they say

And how the adults react,
And, how much food, the kids put away!

Yes, kids can brighten,
Or darken the patrons', day!
But fun to observe, when acting, either way!

As I watched that blue eyed child,
She looked and smiled again,
And we had somewhat of a moment!
Then the mother said,
Don't bother the nice man__

And I winked, and the kid giggled,
And I remembered, then__
Of my children, way back when!

Yes, she with the eyes of vivid blue,
And what a smile,
Could, melt an ice-cold heart__ so true!

Yes always something to catch, my eye,
When at PK's, in the not so early morn!

Ψ

Words to Live by!

If each is to have a life true,
Then all must catch a dream,
And work to follow it through__
For without a dream,
The body atrophies,
As does the mind__
Without our body and mind,
There is little one can do__ but die!
Let this not be you!

Ψ

Ideas Passed!

Listen, and hear me well,
These words I share,
A truth to tell!
No matter, how some would disagree__
Parts of thoughts, someone before has had,
Complete or not, back eons before thee!

Yes, many would like to claim,
A thought or idea was just theirs to name,
But somewhere in the long dark past,
Maybe even a caveman, or a seer,
Or even a sailor man__ that thought, had, had!
That somehow, had, before you had, that's true!

Yes In word, deed, drawing, or in DNA,
From back in yesteryear or millennia,
Humankind has had the idea, in their mind!
And, deny this if you will__
But, you nay, can prove the statement wrong!
Until, you are long dead and gone!

Perhaps, the ownership, is now expired,
And, you are free to work it hard!
And, your name be applied,
As it is found this day,
But remember,
Another makes changes in tomorrow time!

So be wise in your living time,
And, bless the one, perhaps unknown to you!
Whose idea, somehow came on through!
And, also to those, who took the next step on!
And, just maybe, those unborn this day,
A word of gratitude will pass your way!

Consider this, a lesson, free!
And, remember those before,
Truly did in a way, share new &, old ideas,
In a way with you, and even me!
And, gratitude is an inexpensive reward,
For you, as you sign your name into history!

Ψ

Today's, Tomorrow!

The sun this day is shining,
"By God," and the sky is clear,
After days and days of downpour,
Making rivers splash my door!

The sun has deemed to shine,
Tis, time to dry the land!
And, plants to rise once more!

Know, all aspects of life are a circle__
They come, then go and disappear,
And then, with little fanfare,
Come again, their prescience declare!

This is life granted, but note__
To respect and care for Nature!
Is ours to do each day,
If not, one day__
On this earthy rock__
Nothing be there!

Ψ

The Pear Tree!

(A true one, but with, artistic license taken!)

The tree was on a wooded lot,
High above the thoroughfare below,
Not far from the railroad bridge,
That all the kids (mostly boys) did know!

And, on the lot a giant pear tree,
That had seen__
Many generations come and go!
That had a friend of sorts,
Named "Poison Ivy"__
That shared the fallen pears,
When, across the ground did go!

And that tree, posed the question__
Are my pears, worth the itch you get?
That you will have, in weeks to come?

This kept most trespassers,
To a decent flow!
At least__ the very smart ones!

Well, not being the brightest,
Of the lads my same age,
I dined on those big, sweet pears,
And, scratched,
The next few weeks away!

And my poor mother,
Shook her heard in total dismay__
As she washed me head to foot,
With a mixture of alcohol,
And, witch-hazel,
And, whiten me, with,
The lotion calamine, every day!

Well, my grandpa stopped by,
One day to say hello,
And laughed so hard, at the white zombie saw,
So hard, the tears did flow!
I didn't think it was funny,
And he only laughed harder at my call!

When the laughter stopped,
He said, "I see you have been to the
The old pear tree!
That itching, was always, well worth,
The days of scratching,
That had to be for me!"

Then he said: "grandson mine,
I am going share with you a secret,
That my granddad shared with me,
After he that tree did visit__
So many, decades ago to see!"

And, here is what my granddad, told to me!
When in poison ivy or oak__
You find yourself to be__
You can forego all itching or scratching,
With this, "time honored" remedy!

You get a bar of that old time "yellow soap",
Like Octagon or Fells-Naphtha,
And strip those poisoned clothes off,
And they in the washtub go.
Then you get your self in the tub,
Wet full down, not a dry spot to know!

And with that yellow soap,
Give yourself a good wash down,
Then rinse off, and do all again!

That old soap the poison oils will chase,
And, no itching and a scratching for you,
Then only pears, be a memory good and true!

Now I have used that "recipe",
For years that have gone by,
And, I am proud to tell you,
It is the cheapest solution__
And much better than "a poke in the eye!"

Now me, I haven't seen__
That old tree, for many a year!
But, I would give you odds,
That the poison ivy, will find you there!
Then it's yellow soap__ for no itching,
And those pears, you can safely dare!"

Grandpa, has been gone,
For many decades now,
And, I have no idea where,
The secret of "yellow soap"
For such a use they found!

I only wish they had told me,
When out of the cradle, a way I found__
That secret, of the "yellow soap,"
Which, I've passed on, to you now,
Yes, poison oak and Ivy, on earth to stay!
But, old yellow soap__ washes the oils away!

Sort of my legacy, I hope you use, and pass on,
To others, as sort of your dues to pay!

Ψ

Changes!

How strange it seems__
Changes-- enter our lives,
No invitation given__
No door, opened wide!

It is just there,
And, demands you must abide,
Or deny it, and loose__
An opportunity,
Maybe, never again to come by!

Perhaps, it or them,
Do repeat, at a later time?
Perhaps, or maybe not__
Then, too late, for you to cry!

Then again, you might determine__
And, think__ not needed by or for you,
So you shrug, and let it go,
And, the earth rotates,
And around the sun in orbit goes!

Be honest, could we be talking of you?
It sure was me,
When electronics entered the scene,
And, now, there are tears I cry!

So let these words be a lesson,
To give every "change" a fair appraisal,
Not just a passing look!
And, be sure, each change__
Is something, on which, to "set your hook."

Ψ

Life, a Straight Line Not!

What's to eat?
If,Life goes on, in circles found,
Round and round, till living__
Demands, it's ups and downs,
On a path, sometime, a reason finds!

But finding, what is new,
As living runs it's course__
For, it is the "new" that keeps,
Life worth, the time, for breath to take!

And among other things,
It is the breath we take,
That makes, the next__
And, then the next, days worthwhile!

So, look you always,
To things, not yet done,
Or things not even,
Thought yet to be tried__

For they make and keep living, alive!
Know, that success, is to those__
Taking, the "bull" by the horns__
And drag and guide that challenge to be__

On a path that is new born!

Yes, there are times,
When one gets "gored,"
And healing then must be restored!
But, take not your eye off the prize!

For it is with extra effort, then__
One can score, what was surmised!

Life, seldom a straight line,
It is an orbit, the wise do find_
And then the wise,
Steer, a course, on a curving line!
Most times "a pot of gold" will find!

Ψ

Betting Odds!

If there be a war,
Between man and Nature_
Save your money,
And "bet not" on man to win!

The odds are stacked against you!

It would be so smart,
If all humankind, heeded_
The more than hints Nature, provides!
And, not let, his and her stupidity,
Become too much of a destructive tide!

For there are so many,
Lessons, already given_
By each Tsunami and other_
The world has witnessed,

Too bad they have been dismissed,

As only freak happenings provided!
When the message, is clear,
Global Warming, Nature is chiding!

Ψ

Infinity

No one gets out of, life alive!
All should understand that is a truth__
Undeniable, and unchangeable!

Each must do what can be done,
In the time granted__ for a breath to take!
To make each day worth the gift__
Of birth__ others to them gave!

What each and everyone,
Can and must do, is to put forth,
An ongoing sustaining effort__
To make their time on Earth
A value to themselves,
And, to every human,
Who shares this planet too!

No one knows how much good,
Throughout life one can do!
But, each must get up, when down,
And, help others when found__

To make things better,
With each new days sun__
This is a debt, for breath, that comes!

Life is not easy, but it can be as good,
As you most times, can make it!
Just some words,
For you to peruse and in depth review!
As you realize, the gift,
Bestowed, upon you!

Ψ

Life Must Go On!

When we say “Good Bye.”
The pain is real!
Some hurt, you truly feel!

But be aware, and look around!
There be something_
To help ease the pain_ now found!

Surely, you wouldn’t want,
Someone else to catch, the pain you feel_
Then, for them, that pain, will linger on!

You know the one now lost,
Would never truly want,
Their death, for others to bear the cost!

Yes, know, in time the pain, will fade,
And, good memories will remain_
For, that is life, and living is the game to play!

For there is much yet to do!
And those, remaining, must carry through!
Tis a rule of life, this to do!

Life is for the living_
With so much more, always found_
This is the way to honor,
And remember, the one, now gone!

Not with sadness and tears,
But with effort,
To see, a legacy of worth is spun!

Ψ

Song for the Ages!

A ring-a-ding up,
And, a Ring-a-ding down__
And, a Ring-a-Ding__ Ding
All around!
And a Ring-ding in,
And a ring, a ding__ out,
Hear that Pretty Girl__
Give out a shout!

Hold her close__
And, then spin her about,
Ring-a-Ding __ with__
And, a Ring-A-Ding, without__
Climb on a table,
And Dance, all about,
With a Ring-A-Ding, up,
And, a ring-a-ding-down!

All now__ hand in hand!
And, a ring-a-ding together,
No color, ever banned?
For, all are alike__ under the skin,
As, friend and friend,
Across every land!
For, it's, a better world,
When together we win!

So, Ring-A-Ding, Ding, __
And a Ring-A-Ding__ done,
Throughout each night__
Make life great fun!
Tis the only way__
True brotherhood be found,
For each and all, everywhere around!

When Ring-A-Ding Husband,
And Ring-A-Ding wife,
Makes a family better,
All, see, a happier life!
And, this is the story,
Through time _handed down _
So here is, a ring-a-ding wish!
That true brotherhood_ is found!

Ψ

The Gotten!

If all things be equal,
Tomorrow will come,
Be we there or not!
For time goes on, adnauseam!

But, our time_ is measured,
With a final second and date_
Registered only after a life is done!
With ashes gotten,
Or aging bones_
Beneath, God's sea or sun!

So best to offer your thanks,
With each sun that does arise,
That you are privileged_ to see!
Wait not for the last second,
For thanks to give_
For other things might claim,
That last breath from thee!

And your gratitude, lost for eternity!

Ψ

Why Not?

Yes, I know there comes a time,
When all must die!
That is the way of life and living!
But why, must we__
Loose "the bloom of youth__"
And end up, truly old__
In looks and mind__ as we decline,
What would be wrong'
If like one__ of God's snakes,
We shed our old skin,
For a new one__
Before, it's departing time?

And, with a glint in the eye,
Knowing full well,
We were to have a new adventure,
On the other side!
Why would that__ be wrong!

With dignity recalled,
And, pain and frustration gone,
Perhaps could eliminate, the sadness of going__
But go, then with love, and smiles,
And a true excitement found!
What would be wrong with that?
Just some thoughts,
As now__ looking into the mirror on the wall,
And, I need to ask__
Mirror, mirror, once friend of mine,
Who, the devil is that,
I see, staring back at me__
Sure is not the one__ I used to be!

Ψ

Think Ahead!

At times, you wonder, how it happens?
A look away! A blink of the eye!
Then, a wild speeding driver__

And, then the sound of tortured metal!

Twisting, bending in shapes unplanned!
How many times a day__
Is the scenario played, how often displayed?

What is the cost of lives snuffed out__
Of dollars shelled out,
Of sadness and pain laying in wait?

On this day,
The highway, bumper to bumper!
Then, at the "time", the reason unknown__

But the sound, one couldn't deny!
And all sat, as hours__ slipped by!

So thought, might as well settle back__
Scuttlebutt, said two dead__
A compact, now under an 18-wheeler,
Sadness, invaded the scene!

What be the answer?
Is it in driverless cars?
Or is that, just a new challenge to face!

Should we wait, as our world disintegrates?
Or actually, pay heed, for an answer to find?

Ψ

A Place in the Away!

There was a place not long ago,
To visit a friend__ I did go,
Twas a little cross roads town,
Long left behind, when the interstate__
Bypassed, and went around!

Little is left of that town now,
Empty buildings, a filling station,
With a general store,
Just like it was,
More than a century before!

There is something peaceful,
About the surround__
Old farms deserted,
And, few people found,
But hills, and beauty there__ had returned!

I found his place,
Asking a question or two,
It was tucked away,
Not more than a mile or a few,
From that store, where I said howdy-do!

It was an old farmhouse,
More like a cottage, I'd say,
Now that he did spend some time,
Clearing the rot away,
And, fixed it up, and had it, looking fine!

We spent some time,
Reminiscing, of years gone by,
Then, showed me__ to my room,
For the time, I was to stay!
Then put, some fresh fish on the grill!

That afternoon, we walked the grounds,
Up hills, to look at the valleys down!
And, he shared with me the history,
Of a place where, buckskin men,
And American Natives once walked around!

I spent more time there,
Than first I thought I would!
It became part of me,
And, he smiled at me,
For he new this bit of heaven would!

Then some months later,
Back in my place far way,
I received some papers from a lawyer,
With news I never expected that day,
My friend older than I__ had passed away!

Now, I understood better,
Why he showed me all around!
He knew his days were numbered,
And, this land, to me, was to be bound!
A legacy, I not sure, I wanted to have!

Now I spend as much time as I can!
At that cottage in the woodland,
With the spirit, of my old friend!

Just the two of us, his spirit__
And me, feeling like a kid again!

Perhaps someday, I will jot down,
All that took place for me,
In the years, I spent around!
But, for now, I am too busy__
At that cottage, far away, from any crowd!

Ψ

A Thought to Pursue!

There are those,
Who espouse, using "Free Verse!"__
When verse screams for rhyme!
What perhaps those poets__
Don't, and won't understand,
Verse, is the partner__ of music fine!

Good verse,
Tells a story, with every line!
Good verse "sings" to the reader,
And, makes memorable,
Almost every word to find!
Free verse makes for lines unkind!

Is, the writer of free verse__
One__ who is unable to rhyme?
Or is that poet__
Just, deaf, dumb and blind?

Now true to speak,
The previous words, and thoughts
Are just mine,
Although others,
Have indicated to me the same!

Perhaps these words and thoughts,
Are, unkind!
But at least__ they rhyme!
And, will be remembered,
In someone's mind___ sometime!
Maybe?

Ψ

Letter, Unfiled!

I reread a letter this AM__
From an old friend! A friend__
I will most likely never see again!
For we are of the same age,
And, now 3,000 miles apart!
He and his bride in California,
With family! And me' in Delmarva__
Thanking heaven, for each day's start!

My mind goes back to the late sixties__
When we both served together__
Seems a hundred years ago!
In our 20s, with a future ahead!
With, challenges, knocking at the door!
And we, ever ready, to take on more!

And now, so many years have taken flight!
Had always kept in touch,
As changes came, then went!
Each stories, had to live and tell__
But a kinship, had always felt!
And now that tested,
As age and distance, has embarked!

My memories, I can still invoke,
And, I hope, he can, still his do!
And maybe this the best of two worlds,
As two, old life warriors___
Again, facing similar challenges,
Like in times, we once knew!

How strong, the thread friendship bind!

Ψ

Birth Explained!

Life is a gift!
Not requested, but invested!
By strangers, to you unknown!

Their DNA, they sequestered_
Could be on purpose,
Or at the time felt, superfluous!

But later, many times, by some__
Wished it had been divested!
And, certainly, not invested!

But matters not, for you,
Tis now, deposited and hosted__
And then at times, the result is boasted!

Or, rationally accepted!
When in the last trimester,
The female's, body is fully festered!

So, whether seed that made one__
Was either wanted, or unwanted__
Now fully ripened__ is evicted!

Life begins, " that time," has predicted!
Now, you know, some of the history,
Why Earth's population seems uncontested!

But remember, wanted or not__
Your life was gifted!
And, how one uses that gift__ is truly unrestricted!

Ψ

Common Sense Required!

As I sat looking out of windows clear__
Counting the seventeen days,
Till the Equinox will appear!

Crazy weather have seen,
For the last year of more!
Here and everywhere!

Yes, but will say, we here on Delmarva,
Have fared better, than so many others,
Except for rain__ the farmer's bane!
So no moans with you__ will I share!
But prayers, for God's help,
For others__ everywhere!

But for what has happened,
And what is forecast, to come,
Can only say__ only fools today__
Would say, there is,
No Global Warming, "at play"!
And, hopefully__ we have time, to overcome!

If all peoples of the world,
Soon, do not stand together,
As caretakers of the Earth,

And, put their animist aside__
Chances are__ humankind,
A new place, must find to reside!

Or wonder who will be the last,
Into oblivion, slide!

Ψ

Gifted, and Gone!

(A Tribute to so many, who nearly, or passed the century mark!)

Time__ a gift, beyond all measure!
But, know yea, that it is kept!
For each of us, in a history, unknown!
Granted at birth__
With, expiration dates, never shown!
Time, once granted, no more__ known!

Ours to spend, as we best subscribe,
But, once gone,
And our days left behind,
Me-thinks, we are graded__
On how well, we used__ our time!
To better, humankind!

Our life's "Job," is to use that gift of gifts__
For not only ourselves,
But, to better all around!
This is the rent owed by us__
For, days & decades,
We are blessed with breath!

Age is a factor, of how well we use__
Our borrowed time!
For age is a challenge supreme!
Most do, run the race of life,
As a dash, and then think done!

But, it is the time runner,
Who keeps the race alive!
Think of those, we know,
Our sister or brother in life,
Who ran one "peach" of a race!

Well, done, we say__ thanks, "be unto you!"

My "old" friend_ or friends_
Someday to rest, from your Life Long run!
And then, not seen, except on a marker!
She or he out-lived many!

And, in all the years of living,
They granted gifts to humankind_
Gifts, still alive, in those, today survive!
What better legacy could they provide!

Ψ

Life's Lesson!

The fantasy of life,
Keeps and makes, living worthwhile!
For, without dreams,
Life is but a trial!

When too much,
Anger and frustration felt_
Then, lifted, in the air!
A losing proposition expressed_
With fewer chances,
A smile to capture then!

The answer is in every head!
So dream much, and dream big_
Make plans, and work,
To make life_ worthwhile!
Doing so, and "God," will smile!

Ψ

In Memories Find!

Not long ago, a nephew died,
And, his "tapestry" is now done!
His death, followed by 18 months,
His younger brothers' trip beyond!

The first by ALS, fast!
That, fortunately, was not long in time!
The second, when a car,
His motorcycle took the right away from!

Neither had reached their 60th year,
Both, gone far too soon!
Too much talent did disappear!
Too much living, yet to be done!

All lives, an expiration date__ have,
This I have been told,
And we, of the humankind,
Are not privileged that date to know!

I miss these, no longer boys,
That I had the gift to know,
But, watched them in their younger years,
As talent bloomed, and in times did grow!

Tis a shame we talent can't bottle,
To pass on to an heir,
Perhaps then the loss less hard__
When one, is no longer here!

So in time, make lasting memories,
That you can call on, to return,
And they will live through you,
Till your candle, no longer burns!

The good and bad of living long_
Is, that breath you still, can grab!
But, the loss you must endure,
When those you no longer have!

So walk not away, from moments,
When for seconds another memory,
Can be got!
For it may be the last, and you know not!

Fare-thee-well, my nephews,
For you I do morn_
Until, perhaps, we meet again,
In another place and time!

Ψ

A Thought to Remember!

Nature abhors a vacuum!

Thus when there is a loss_
And you no more than look around,
Taking time for sight and sound_

That vacuum cannot be found!
And, what is new or a replacement,
Maybe, even better now!

But, if recall, miss what once known to all!

Ψ

Still Time to Hear!

It was one of those mornings,
The heat and humidity down!
The widows, open, and the fans on!
The air conditioner, "on switch", not found!

A little housework to attend,
So on the Bose,
I, put a favorite, I can't__
When on the IMac, time I must spend!

For when that disc I hear,
I just want to move and shake,
Not a new disc__
Well__ read and see the reasoning I make:

How did I miss so much?
I now, listen to the talent,
Of, my days 40 years by,
And, wonder how, now gone, and why?

Their, music that now, touches my soul!
Where was I, when it was fresh and new?
Did time I waste, those years gone by?
Seeing "The Last Waltz", my sadness grew!

Now 40 years hence, "the Band," now gone__
Four decades thence!
That live talent, lost to time!
Only their music, now, captured in my mind!

First they the "Hawk", then as "The Band."
Their reputation recognized by many!
But unfortunately not by me!
And now long gone, only on disc I find,

There sound to hear and see!
A treasure, to the ear,
To the body and one's mind!
An outstanding time to find!

Now remembered, as ABBA by name,
What music, what rhythm,
What voices four, built the fame!
You hear them play and sing,
As fresh remembered, the mind does replay!

Why does talent, move far astray?
Men and women, both married,
Then split, then, go on their way!
Their music alive; still__
Almost half century, many play!

Listen, listen, you can hear the beat!
It stirs your soul, and moves your feet!
It's ABBA, an entity, theirs alone!
Gone are the tours__
Now, only on CD's, the talent shown!

And the music, in two movies now!
Do you have feelings somewhat the same?
I think not, that in this I am alone!
Amazed am I__ how music on one does grow!

Ψ

Off Times: we take the good for granted,
And, saying thanks, we forget__
When thanks, cost so little, and means so much!

Ψ

Wistful Thoughts!

Perhaps there comes that time,
When minds, should erase,
Some__ passages from the past!

Many times those great memories,
Are gone with no chance to return!

And now, it is, almost impossible,
For one, to try to paint, for another__
A picture of that time and place!

And, you know, there are not enough,
Colors on your pallet, to bring them__
To life, in this new day and time!

Many times you realize, to try__
Is to suffer, an overwhelming sadness,
Of a memory now harder to find!

Tis a moment when,
A chasm opens,
And, the teller (you), truly realizes__

These are your memories,
Hopefully to be shared__
But, missed the mark, and frustrations bear!

Great memories, I now opine—
Should be written down,
At, or near the happening time!

When details of action__
Color, place, and who; is fresh in mind!
And, if photos attached would be fine!

Then, in a future time,
Let the writing and hopefully more,
Backup your story line!

Particularly if like me__
You are not an oral.
Telling machine!

Oh, to be like the Irish,
When it comes, to story relating__
Where, they are just sublime!

But, me I am not Irish__
And, maybe should not share memories,
Is a better idea__ than fine?

Or share with only others, who think,
My telling is just fine!
Or, in verse, write some lines!

Ψ

A Thought to Subscribe!

"Keep the Faith!
Is, more than just words__
It is a "State of Mind!"

Brought forth (me thinks) by those,
With the tenacity, to survive!
And, give all a try, in time!

Sounds, as though, this all should try!

Ψ

A Boat of Size!

That, " O'Day" I sold in '77,
As I moved, to another state!
But, did get to sail with others__
And when, in illness, bought from a friend__
His "Freedom," to start the new millennium!

I soloed quite a lot,
And, at times, felt my dad was at the helm!
There is much more to that story,
But that is for another time to tell!

Perhaps, my days of sailing__
Now left to the years before,
But not my love of boats,
Nor that of the Chesapeake__
My muse, from the time, I was a boy!

I live close to a river now,
Which I see most everyday!
It's tidal current ebbs and flows__
And helps me, remember those other days!

I hope your memories stand the test of time,
And your dreams__ you never set aside!
And, even better, than dreams__

Did make memories,
As you, threw your duffel on board,
Up anchored, and then sailed away__
With the tide!

Ψ

Whose There?

Houses, many, span, unnumbered generations,
But, many times__ most times,
The new tenant knows little or nothing,
Of those that walked the halls__
Before they, the house was theirs!

Too bad__
What history, and context unknown!
What rationale for this or that,
Could better be understood!

What secrets come to light!
Then again,
To, stay or run away, in fright!
Questions__ make living a delight!

Oh, if a house, could only talk!

Ψ

Boater's Prayer!

As those in awe, of the waters around us,
And of the boats who kiss the waves,
For the bounty you have placed before us,
May it, give us strength on our way__

We ask, you bless our time on earth,
And accept our gratitude and praise!
We humbly ask, you, to hear our prayer,
And let service - fill our days!
Amen!

Ψ

A Difference Make!

I was chatting with a man one day,
A man I met on a park bench,
Along life's way!

A man once, unknown to me,
A man of years & learned wisdom!
This I understood, with first words,
We exchanged__ that's true!

"Do you have a minute or two,'
Young man, he said?
And I nodded saying "I certainly do!"

He then smiled and said these words:
"And, I guarantee if you listen closely,
They will be worth much to you."

"If you but believe,
And with effort put them to work,
They will make a difference,
In living your life!"

"They will, help make all of your days,
The best they can be!
Accept them as your motto__
And get your mind to agree!"

And now, I pass his words along to you,
Just four words: but true:
"I can do it!"

"If with effort try__
These four, you daily bring to the fore,
In all that you do__"

"Mean what you say,
And, full effort, to carry them through,
Then success will be yours__
Until no more breath__ yours will be"

"Now, I am not saying,
Each effort, a success attained__
For that the way in life will never be!
But, more than you can imagine,
Will paint rosy, each sunrise you see!"

"Yes, use those four words,
Garner information required,
To carry them through,"

"Do not fail them,
And, they will not fail you!

Believe what I say,
And find the best in life you can do!"

His words then finished,
Then believe it or not,
A horse drawn carriage,
Through the park, did come!

He stood, waved his hand,
And got aboard, smiled and waved again,
And off the horse and driver went__
Disappearing with the evening sun!

Now I never saw, that man again__
But one day, a letter to me came!
From him__ I did receive!
And thought, how can this be?

For he was old then,
When in the park we met__
And, many years from then, had fled by me!

And, it was dated like a few days before,
And the message was simple,
And straight to the point!

"You, **done good__** my once young friend!
For, I have been watching you.

And now, its time for you__
To pass those words, to another someone young!"

- - - -

And, this is why, on this day,
I shared them with you!
And, if I could do__ so can you!
Just a thought or two__
That will make your life, better for you!

"You can do it!"

Yes, all you need do,
Is live those four words:

I can do it!

And, work toward that goal,
And, more than "never", they will be true!

This, be my Legacy to you!

Ψ

"Salad Days!"

Long gone are my "salad days!"
When every moment, an exercise__
To reach out__
For the next big thing to come!

When it mattered not,
If it was a fight to defy gravity,
Or a sport, the champ, to take on,
Or catching a date with the "elusive one!"
And now__ here I sit,
In a chair that with little effort rocks,
Just waiting for the next meal to come!
Or, a change__ long overdo!

What in the heck happened,
To my life, that was mine, only yesterday?
And, who are these old ones,
Filling up this porch in the sun!

Oh my God, I've gotten old!
What did I do to deserve this?
Then the old broad sitting next to me said:
"You lived, too damn long!
"Too long", shouts I__ "why, I'm only___"
"A hundred and four," says she!
"He, he hee, and you're younger than me!"

"Holly Cow", says I__
"What are we waiting for?"
Says she: "for the Devil to get his fill,
And then it's "Heaven" for you and me!"
And, we both laughed!

Ψ

Verbiage!

I couldn't believe__
They were that big!
I swatted one,
And, I swear a quart of blood,
Splattered everywhere!

Well, maybe not a quart__
But there was more than a lot!
That "mother",
Must have had a wingspan, of 747!

Now I had heard stories of these skitters,
From old timers of the Maine woods!

And, like most thought,
They were just that,
Tales to impress the tenderfoot!
Well, dammit, they were true!

I watch a half dozen or so,
Pick up a two-man canoe,
With two fat guys on board!

And, head for the deep woods!
Where they could take their time,
Removing any trace of Type "A", positive!

Well the guys escaped,
30 pounds lighter,
And sort of a pale ashen color!

Running as fast as they could__
For the New Hampshire border!
God's truth! Why would I lie to you?

At night, thank heaven for the campfire,
For there was no moon light,
Too many of them out,

That they blocked that satellite!
And, if you weren't fast enough,
To get away,
Oh, I can't even tell you what they would do!

I know, I know__
You think I'm pulling your leg!

But, why does__
The Maine Legislature__
Have bounty on each one you kill?
Yes, 85 cents for each body shown!
And, that is cash money!

Now, you can stop laughing!
But, come on up to Maine,
For a great vacation!

And, even donate,
A quart of fresh blood!
And, earn some money!

And, the lobsters are truly great!
Hope to see you "down east"!

Just a little humor__
From a coed, Explore Post__
That spent 11 summers
Canoeing the Allagash
And, loving every minute of it!

Ψ

Retrospective__ I Believe

Should, a day go by,
And, a Verse__ I have not __

Inked, and written down__
That to me, is a bad day__
For me__ to ever recall!

For I look, for those thoughts,
To enter my mind__
Of lines, stories and tales__
For them to always come__
But, from whence, I know not where!

But, most times, they are there!
And there am I.

With a burning desire,
To pen in ink on paper, those words__
That have, been to me__ supplied!

Could it be a reason never known__
A gift__ found in a dream,
That I__ have received?
And this, a mission, I am to do?
I don't know, if, this be true!

But, I will write and write,
As long as I am able to!

For if this, I cannot do__
I then feel, a day of breathing lost__
For an effort, I was tasked__ but by whom?

These are but my thoughts__ sane or not?
But, stranger things__
In this world others have "gotten!"

Could, this come from an entity_
Not known, playing games, on my lot!

Am I to know, or never not:
If, this, a gift from God_
Or just one of Satin's_ goulash plots?
Or, does it really matter_
As long, as verse, to me, I get, or got!

Oh well, I am here, like it or not!

Ψ

Parting of the Ways!

Divorce: many times deserved,
Other times unearned,
Sometimes welcomed! Many times spurned!

And at other times, too late!
Sometimes, after time_
Back with the same spouse,
Together, but never marriage found!

Marriage, like "Boot Camp" all over again!
And then again, the best decision ever made!
Neither, guaranteed_
To be: assured, insured or ensured!

"Just a roll of the dice in life; think you, the same?

Ψ

"Time in a Bottle!"

If one would ask me which was_
My, all time favorite movie,
The list would be so very long!

For, I could not name just one!
But one of the many, would be:
"St. Elmo's Fire!"

Most likely not yours,
But mine because it touched on_
Times I would have_

Liked to have shared,
With the generation, after, my own!

Now get me not wrong,
For, I truly loved my time, growing_

During, the last of the 1930s into 50s!
That was a special time, indeed!

But St. Elmo's Fire_
Touched on a time,
When things and life,
Were, not unlike, the 1920s,
After the "War to End all Wars!

A cast of then young actors,
Made their roles come alive_
In a portrait they painted!

As today looking back,
Spelled an era, good and bad,
Of a moment, in history had!

Each time I see, that work, on the screen,
Oh, yes I have watched it a time or more__
I can see myself, for a moment or two__

In that life experience, I never had!
And today, I am glad__ tis only a dream,
To chance, a moment to tour!

It is funny, how most__
Of wishes to relive,
Are of times in history past!

But times of "St. Elmo's Fire,"
Were times, of youth, living ahead__
Too late for me, ever to recast!

Yes, tis a favorite movie of mine,
And, treats me to another time,
Not to have had!

But now, a bit older and wiser,
Makes me wonder,
If it's full impact, even today can grab?

Perhaps, It's time to review,
Your favorite or favorites,
That on film demands a return!

Then to touch, a moment you too have?
Like me, keep dreaming, what if__
But glad, it but a dream unknown!

Oh, to put a time of life in a bottle,
And, seal it, for a time to come__
To be uncorked, when__ life seems undone!

Ψ

Hear the Notes!

The music from the Bose was Vermont made__
The folk sound, for this day was right!
Feelings strong as I read, each line,
Editing my latest book, a challenge__
But a feeling grand inside!

Never thought, I a book in print make!
But, here now readying number ten__
And while the words keep coming,
Verse, I will continue to write!
My prayer, for readers to try!

For that is what I strive to do!
When before sunrise, me at my MAC__
Can on most days always be found!
Yes, I write as a legacy for family,
And, all humankind!

This I will do as long as am able,
With rhyming words, formed in my mind!
And they tell short stories of worth,
That I pray and hope__
Can help all, with these words to find!

This be__ a talent, that bloomed late!
And, at times finds__ me hoping__
As I, sign and sell books, all a value to share__
A legacy, for my family, I craft!
And for organizations, the profit is theirs!

Verse, songs from my soul, but notes, I can't write!

Ψ

A Life Worth the Time!

How is your life's Tapestry, coming along?
Is truth woven in every warp and fill?

Or is your ego coloring every line!
To distort the story, others will find!

How will future generations,
View the life that you__ wove each day!
As truth or lies__ what will history say?

You know, if all worked for__ perfection,
Little discoloration in your "Life Tapestry,"
Others, would look, too hard to find!

Remember, your tapestry,
Is the legacy you leave behind!

It speaks not only of you,
But, of the ancestors,
"Whose DNA, you carry down the line!

Yes, think of your life as a tapestry__
To be seen for a long time!
For then, you might care what others find!

One will note any lies__
In garish colors,
Disturbing the flow of story lines!

Do your best, to weave a good life!
If you do, your legacy should be fine!

And maybe__ you will be missed over time!

Ψ

No Regrets!

Regrets__ how can I have them__
When borne with breath,
And received, years to run!

Matters not, I saw not more__
For, what seen, was mine to store,
To put away in my mind!
And then to recall in memories__
In color vivid and fine!

Of course, more__
Could have done and seen__
But, I am me__ and not__
Another's life to live__
Regrets, how can I proclaim!

If I didn't try for more__
Then to me goes the shame!
But I saw—me thinks,
All I wanted to see!
In the time, that was for me__
At that time to see!

Perhaps, if I thought a bit, Just maybe some more,
Would have liked to see__
But, I know, there was just enough time,
For me to see__ all I did see!

Perhaps, there is a second life to come__
Or, even more, before I'm done__
And even then, if I didn't,
See it all__
I think not, have regrets, even then!

For I am me!

And even with a second life or more__
How much can one see, if one won't see?
For each is a vessel, whose space__
Will accept a cargo, willing it to be!

Regrets maybe for you, but not for me!
For with words, a tapestry,
In my mind I paint__
And hope, it a legacy__ for those to follow me!

How much better, can life be?

Ψ

Lack of Understanding!

Tis a shame__
Too many decades wasted away!
By misunderstanding, and undeserved hate!
For others, that we truly don't know!
Which cost, each, and everyone, of us__
The best in life__ that could be!

If, only, with selective blindness__
Together, not see race, gender, creed or color,
Or anything that pulls people apart!
Then the whole world__
Would a better place be!

Division__ is the Devil's game,
Let's all, on God's team play!
And take the time,
To recognize__ everyone,
For the good that each can display!

Ψ

Boots & Brushes!

A fisherman in mid-stream,
Cast his fly, with practice shown__
Dropping it some 60 feet away!

And then played,
The casting game,
Recast, and worked his lure!

Soon he got his first strike!
And then, played the fishing game,
Bringing a good size trout,
Into, his net employed!

I watched him,
It seemed for an endless time!
Enjoying, the action,
Of the game!
And his success,
As fish, after fish his net did claim!

He took a break,
And waded to shore,
To set his rod down,
I offered him a cup of "Joe!"

Then over a cup or two,
Each other got to know!
Of the weather, fishing and art!

It seemed we had mutual friends,
But he and I,
Never before did know!
Strange how life seems to go!

Then back to casting his lure,
And me, some more paint,
With brush on canvas spread,
Till the sun,
Began to drop, below the horizon line!

Together, up the path we trod,
Chatting all the way,
Planned, we did to meet again,
A new friendship__ was at play!

He bid me wait a time,
And for two cups of coffee__
We had shared,
Two fine trout, he gifted me!

Me, I shared with him a look,
At, the fisherman,
On the canvas, almost done,
That was a mirror image of he!

And, when in time I finished it,
In my studio at home,
Presented it to him,
And, that was now, many years ago!

Shared coffee, trout and art,
And two, who became great friends!
How better to spend a life,
Before life comes to an end!

Let not your reluctance or fear,
Stop you from a chance meeting__
You never know, when a new friend, find!

Ψ

Deep Thought a Demand!

The car it crashed,
After, a hard, hard run,
Was it, an accident?
Or, perhaps, an ending, just begun!

Life is good, but a challenge all the way!
Sometimes, living gets in the way,
Pressure, stress, illness,
Changes the game__ being played!

Many think they know the answer__
But is that really true?
In a life, full of chaos_
Some; would death rather choose!

But, thank heaven__ that is only a few!
But still, too many__
With talent, gone too soon!
Perhaps, a good listener, an option to choose!

Thus, talking out a problem__
Understanding, what words, placed in the air__
Can lead to clearer thinking__
That living__ is the choice to choose!

Ψ

In a Name!

Throughout the vicissitudes of life!
Not all can catch the "faith!"
But many are able to!
You could call them__
Thrivers!

Ψ

Make Worth Your Goal!

It is the days in your life__
And the living of your days__
That makes each day,
And, your life__ worthwhile!

Worthwhile, is the eternal quest__
Of living a life!
For, without life being worthwhile,
Why live life at all?

The world, unfortunately,
Is full of worthless living things__
That take up God's__
Space, breath and time!

But, fortunately, there is "worth",
To be seen and gathered,
Throughout life__ for the agile mind!
Worthlessness, is mostly__
Laziness, personified!

Stand-up and put all laziness aside!
Become worth the time you are alive!
For when you do,
This is your legacy's__ payment for time had!

Ψ

God has a way__ And, a reason, for slowing us down__
This, is why, he/she invented sofas!
So one__ is near, when stumbling around,
A dream place, each day__ to be found!

Ψ

Gifting a Purpose!

One of our jobs in life,
Is to assure we use,
That marvelous gift from birth!

That of, the breath of life__
For not only our benefit,
But, for all humankind!

This is the rent we owe,
For the moments, days and decades,
We are blessed with living!

Age, is one of the factors,
Of, how well,
We use our borrowed time!
For as we age,
One has the opportunity__
To use even better__ time!

Know that you are being judged__
By all, who are everywhere around!
But, an even harder judge__ is you, yourself!

Judgment is a subjective thing__
Recognizing it or not__
We always are__ being judged!

As we, are always judging others!
Use it, for the betterment of all,
Not as punitive, but for good!

Ψ

Once Known!

Now, that I admit,
I have, reached my elder years__
I do truly appreciate more,
Those older ones with hair of grey__
And with slower gate__

Those, in the day, had known!
Whom I then thought, out of step in time!
As the young today, think of me!

I only wish, I could recapture,
The time and wisdom__
I could have gained, and let skip by!
Had I only, been wise enough,
To sit at the feet__
Of the elders__ I once knew!

Oh, how I wish this day,
I had the power to hold,
Today's youth, and share__
Much that__ could, serve them well,
With, no loss felt, in decades to come!

I fear, this is a lack,
That will in no generation, see a cure!
For in the time of youth,
There is no time__ to fully see,
The future, yet to come!

Too bad, wisdom, is wasted on the old__
Or should say,
Wisdom, not accepted, by the young!

Ψ

I Hurt for the Earth!

My heart exists in sadness,
As I watch erosion and subsidence,
And the stupidity of my fellow man!

As he and she, disabuse,
This Eden__ this planet Earth,
That all should be nurturing,
For the generations, yet to come!

And little can I do!
But think how much could be done,
If humankind, all would pitch in__
And, truly see __ the experiment fully run!

If one would look at the planets
Our neighbors in the sky!
One could hardly miss the fact_
That Earth was especially chosen!

Chosen, for an experiment, with humankind!
But, unless things change with rapidity__
Tis obvious, the experiment will end and die!
I wonder, how many will let tears "fly?"

Ψ

Being

I can never be you,
But being you, I never want to be!
I would like to share your talents,
And, always hold your respect,
And, best of all,
Hope you think the same of me!

Ψ

A Question?

What fools, be humankind,
When in an almost, Eden__
We plot the perfect crime!
That thing called WAR!
When talent we bury,
With few tears to find!
And cannot wait,
For the next WAR to find!

Why I ask, are there always a few__
Who for whatever reason, only live for WAR?
Why is it, this sickness__ we cannot cure?

Ψ

Truth!

"In justice," we grow to be!
Most times all we can!
"With, injustice," a living death,
Is, what is ahead of thee!
Justice they say is "Blind!"
How and why is Justice sightless!

When justice, is the best part, of humankind!
How can some be so bad and wicked__
And treat fellow humans as they do__
And think them selves, just?

Justice at all times,
Is the true measure of humankind!
If so__ then what does that say,
About this world, of yours and mine__
When justice, many times__ is left behind?

Ψ

Never Alone!

Believe you__ not in God?
You are certainly not alone!
But whether you are right or wrong__
Understand, for to believe,
Much must be assumed!

For seldom does God,
Speak directly to you!
But, look you around__
And, see those many things,
In this world, that science does explain,
But not "how" they truly came!

And that **"why"** should give you pause!
Could there be __ "A" God?

Yes, belief requires faith,
And agreed, faith is a taskmaster__
That clouds many a mind!
However; seems pretty smart to me,
Why a chance take__
When God (a he or she), you call upon,
When in trouble, you find!

The old saying:
"No atheists__ do you find__ in foxholes!
Just those calling on "God!"
When, this world is at War!
Maybe it is time "for all" to find God"!
Or at least as the Bible says__
"Do unto others, The Golden Rule,
May give you time to decide!!

Ψ

Full Stop, a Dream?

What today, seems out of place__
One day will be commonplace!
As seeing the sunrise_
In a “good morning “ shout!
As natural as breathing in and out!

So perhaps__ fear, concern and challenge
Is, a nod to acknowledge__
The people of the world,
Will not and cannot, stand still!
For all must adapt, to movement forward!

Even though at times, sitting quiet be the wish!
But being still, is a warrant of demise!
So move along__ life is too short anyway,
Just know, that forward__
Fortunately or unfortunately is: “The Way!

Ψ

Appraisal!

I am not an oral story-teller__
I wish I were! I am not a speech giver__
And would rather and did.
Write, for others__ my words to give!

But, I do have some small talent,
To put on paper, words in verse!
Words that could be, for my obituary?
Don’t get your hopes up__ I feel fine!

Ψ

Gracious Gifts!

For each Season that you grant us!
For each day that we arise!
For the many gifts that you bestow upon us!
For the beauty of earth and sea, and sky!

For our share of daily sustenance,
For others to share the same!
For family and friends gathered round us!
For all a chance to play "life's game!"

For your hand upon our shoulder,
May your forgiveness always endure!
Ask we, you to guide our journey,
For whatever Life has in store!

For food upon our tables,
For this and blessings more!
We thank you heavenly Father,
Help us, your will to ensure!
Amen!

Ψ

FINIS

www.ingramcontent.com/pod-product-compliance
Lightning Source LLC
Chambersburg PA
CBHW060204050426
42446CB00013B/2989
* 9 7 8 1 6 2 8 0 6 3 0 5 9 *